LIVING LEGENDS OF SPORTS

NEYMAR

SOCCER SUPERSTAR

MARTY GITLIN

Britannica Educational Publishing

IN ASSOCIATION WITH

ROSEN EDUCATIONAL SERVICES

Published in 2019 by Britannica Educational Publishing (a trademark of Encyclopædia Britannica, Inc.) in association with The Rosen Publishing Group, Inc.
29 East 21st Street, New York, NY 10010

Distributed exclusively by Rosen Publishing.
To see additional Britannica Educational Publishing titles, go to rosenpublishing.com.

First Edition

Britannica Educational Publishing
J.E. Luebering: Executive Director, Core Editorial
Andrea R. Field: Managing Editor, Compton's by Britannica

Rosen Publishing
Kathy Kuhtz Campbell: Senior Editor
Nelson Sá: Art Director
Nicole Russo-Duca: Series Designer and Book Layout
Cindy Reiman: Photography Manager
Sherri Jackson: Photo Researcher

Library of Congress Cataloging-in-Publication Data

Names: Gitlin, Marty, author.
Title: Neymar : soccer superstar / Marty Gitlin.
Description: New York: Britannica Educational Publishing, in Association with Rosen Educational Services, 2019. | Series: Living Legends of Sports | Includes bibliographical references and index. | Audience: Grades: 5–8.
Identifiers: LCCN 2017050390| ISBN 9781538302149 (library bound) | ISBN 9781538302156 (paperback)
Subjects: LCSH: Neymar, 1992—Juvenile literature. | Soccer players—Brazil—Biography—Juvenile literature.
Classification: LCC GV942.7.N455 G57 2019 | DDC 796.334092 [B] —dc23
LC record available at https://lccn.loc.gov/2017050390

Manufactured in the United States of America

Photo credits: Cover, p. 1 TF-Images/Getty Images; cover and interior pages background © iStockphoto/traffic_analyzer; pp. 4-5 Dave Winter/Icon Sport/Getty Images; p. 6 © iStockphoto.com/diegograndi; pp. 7, 36-37 Jean Catuffe/Getty Images; pp. 8-9, 32 Ricardo Nogueira/AFP/Getty Images; p. 11 Stanley Chou/Getty Images; p. 12 Tim Clayton/Corbis Sport/Getty Images; p. 15 Stuart Franklin /FIFA/Getty Images; p. 16 Luis Vera/LatinContent WO/Getty Images; p. 17 AFP/Getty Images; pp. 18-19 Laurence Griffiths /Getty Images; p. 20 Quique Garcia/AFP/Getty Images; pp. 23, 24, 34 David Ramos/Getty Images; pp. 25, 31 Anadolu Agency /Getty Images; pp. 26-27 Martin Bernetti/AFP/Getty Images; p. 29 Lionel Bonaventure/AFP/Getty Images; p. 35 Matthew Ashton-AMA /Getty Images.

CONTENTS

INTRODUCTION

Neymar da Silva Santos Jr. is like a magician. Not the kind of magician that can pull a rabbit out of a hat. He is like a magician with a soccer ball. Neymar can do things with his favorite toy that fans would not believe is possible.

Opposing players wish they were impossible. But they have seen it with their own eyes. They have been fooled by the amazing ballhandling of the Brazilian star as he burns them for goal after goal.

Neymar is perhaps the greatest soccer player in the world. It is no wonder that Spanish soccer club FC Barcelona spent millions of dollars to lure him from his home country. And it is no wonder that the French club Paris Saint-Germain spent millions to pry him away from FC Barcelona.

Both clubs fully understood that Neymar could do more than help their teams win. He would also be embraced by their fans for his incredible skills.

Yet Neymar is more than just a great soccer player. He is a father. He is among the highest-paid athletes in the world of advertising. He is a generous person who loves kids. His charity work in Brazil has helped the children of that country live better lives.

Neymar has emerged as a superstar. It all started with an encouraging father, a love for the sport, and a gift for soccer.

Neymar prepares to move downfield in a 2017 match. His amazing balance and ballhandling are considered his greatest assets.

Fly
Emirates
PARIS

CHAPTER ONE

The Boy Wonder

It was 1998. Soccer scout Betinho dos Santos was searching for talent in the Brazilian town of São Vicente. He watched some players booting a ball around the beach.

He knew a gifted athlete when he saw one. After all, only a few years before, he had discovered a future superstar in Robinho. But the most intriguing prospect he observed that day was not running around on the sand. He was hanging around his mother in the stands.

Soccer is popular at Santos Beach in the Brazilian town of São Vicente. Neymar's talents were discovered there as a six-year-old.

Dos Santos might never have imagined finding a potential star in any six-year-old. Yet there he was—a skinny little kid performing magic with a soccer ball. Dos Santos stared at the child. The more he stared, the more amazed he became.

That was a moment dos Santos would never forget. "I saw that kid running around and he caught my attention," he recalled later during an interview. "He already had agility and coordination. Of course, he was very, very thin too. Then he started doing some tricks with the ball, tricks that a normal kid would never do. I was shocked."

QUICK FACT

Neymar was born and raised near one of the biggest cities in the world. Only four cities have more people than São Paulo, Brazil. The population of São Paulo's metropolitan area was more than 21 million in 2016. That represents the largest population of any city in the Western Hemisphere.

That child was Neymar da Silva Santos Jr. Among the professional players on the beach that day was his father, Neymar da Silva Sr. His

Neymar (*right*) and his father (*center*) watch a soccer match. Neymar's dad instilled a passion for soccer into his son at an early age.

dad had instilled in him a passion for soccer that would remain for a lifetime. The boy needed little encouragement. He showed an interest in the sport at the age of two.

The younger Neymar was born in Mogi das Cruzes on February 5, 1992. The town is a short drive north from São Paulo, the largest city in Brazil. He moved at age six with his family to his grandmother's home in São Vicente, a beach town just south of São Paulo.

Neymar would not stay there long. His father did not play soccer at near the level his son would. Neymar would sign a contract with teams that gave him a chance. The next move was to Jardim Gloria, an area in the city of Praia Grande.

The family was not rich. But it was wealthier than any other in

QUICK FACT

Neymar's sister, Rafaella Beckran, is a successful model. Neymar and Rafaella are very close. They even sport matching tattoos. His reads *sorella*, which means "sister" in Italian. Hers reads *fratello*, which translates to "brother" in Italian.

Neymar was raised as one of the luckier children in the Jardim Gloria neighborhood. The area is part of the town of Praia Grande.

Jardim Gloria. Neymar's family lived in one of its best houses. Many of Neymar's friends resided in shacks. Other kids were fortunate to have many toys. Neymar boasted a collection of 50 soccer balls. He also owned a video game that made him the envy of his neighbors.

Planting the Seeds for a Career

Most important to Neymar was that his home was close to Santos. That is the Brazilian soccer club made famous by the legendary Pelé. He was perhaps the greatest player ever. It was with Santos that Neymar would begin his brilliant career.

Not that Neymar lacked confidence before he joined Santos in 2003. The boy played with swagger even when he first started booting a ball around as a toddler.

Soon after discovering Neymar, the soccer scout dos Santos began taking him to play futsal. Futsal is a brand of indoor soccer that places an emphasis on basic skills. Neymar displayed incredible dribbling and shooting abilities. His talents were quickly noticed. Brazilian soccer standout José Ely de Miranda, known as Zito, brought Neymar to Santos. Neymar signed his first contract with the club at age 11.

The boy had needed little help in gaining a passion for the sport. The encouragement he received from his family was already reaping rewards. His father recognized the delight with which his son played the game. He inspired his child to pursue his dreams.

"The soccer pitch is Neymar Jr.'s joy," said his father. "If you give him a soccer field he'll be happy. It doesn't matter where it is ... That's what allows Neymar to keep his joy."

His father believed young Neymar would pursue a professional career from the moment he joined Santos. He honed his skills against much older competition. Spanish soccer clubs such

QUICK FACT

The young Neymar was given the nickname Juninho. That means "Junior" in Portuguese, Brazil's official language.

Brazil competes in many futsal championships, such as this one in 2003. The indoor sport helps athletes improve their basic soccer skills.

as Barcelona and Real Madrid were already taking interest in the talented youngster. They knew that any player who signs a contract before his teenage years must boast great talent.

Real Madrid saw that talent firsthand in 2005. That is when Neymar traveled to Madrid to try out for its Merengues youth program. It is believed he was immediately accepted. But Santos was not about to let Neymar go. Brazilian club president Marcelo Teixeira gave Neymar's father more than $1 million to keep his son with Santos.

Becoming a Star

Neymar remained with Santos. He made his debut with the club at age 17 on March 7, 2009. He scored his first goal a week later in a Santos victory. He helped the team win the league championship in 2010.

A young Neymar shows off his skills in a 2010 match. He was well on his way to becoming the premier player in his native country of Brazil.

Santos soon became known as the "Boys of the Village" for the talented players it had groomed in recent years. Neymar and teammates such as Robinho and Paulo Henrique Ganso were emerging stars.

Neymar was the best of all. The forward led the league with 11 goals later in 2010 to help Santos win the Brazilian Cup. He had further impressed European scouts. It was believed that only the intervention of Pelé prevented Neymar from signing with the British club Chelsea. The soccer legend convinced Neymar to stay with Santos.

The year was not all rosy for Neymar. He was left off the 2010 Brazilian World Cup team that was to compete in South Africa. Dunga, the head coach of Brazil's national team, claimed that the 18-year-old was simply not ready. Those that had seen Neymar in action disagreed.

Neymar claimed when asked about it before the 2014 World Cup that he had not been disappointed. He accepted the decision at the time.

"It was not my turn (then) to play a World Cup," he said. "I have always worked for this day—unfortunately it didn't happen for me on that occasion. But after that I was lucky enough to be called up to wear the Brazilian colors."

He could not be held back much longer. Neymar was about to emerge as one of the superstars of soccer.

CHAPTER TWO

Onward and Upward

Neymar was considered the best player in Brazil by 2011. He was soon added to its national team. And he continued to star for Santos.

He scored one of the winning goals to lead Santos to its first Libertadores Cup (the most prestigious South American club competition) title in 48 years. He earned the Puskás Award for scoring the best goal of the year. That goal against Flamengo on July 27, 2011, is still considered by many his greatest ever. Neymar set it up by bolting past two defenders. Three other defenders converged. He faked out the closest one by stopping the ball with his right foot and slipping it past him with the left. He then blasted it past the sprawling goalkeeper. "Sensational!" screamed the announcer as the amazed fans in the stands screamed their approval.

But Neymar and Santos were humbled in Switzerland in January 2012. They played European powerhouse Barcelona in a Club World Cup match. The result was a 4–0 defeat that showed how inferior his team was to the best in the world.

Neymar knew now that he had to play with the best to become the best. It would not be long before the Barcelona team that had crushed Santos would become his team as well.

Neymar had proved himself all he could for Santos. In 2011, he averaged nearly a goal a game, which is virtually unheard of at the

Neymar proudly displays the FIFA Puskás Award he earned in 2011. The honor is presented to the soccer player who scored the most impressive goal of the year.

Neymar boots the ball during Libertadores Cup action in 2011. His achievements in that competition helped earn him South America Footballer of the Year honors.

higher levels of soccer. He was a dynamo at 5 feet 9 inches and 150 pounds. He displayed amazing body control, quick reflexes, and incredible acceleration and speed.

In 2011, after leading his team to its first Libertadores Cup since 1963, Neymar kneeled and cried. He then spoke about what he considered his greatest thrill as a player. "It's the happiest day of my life, I made history," he said.

More Goals, More Awards

Neymar earned South America Footballer of the Year honors that year and the next. The awards came as no surprise. In 2012, he scored 23 goals in 31 matches in league and Libertadores Cup action. He added another 20 goals in 16 state championship events and nine more in 11 national matches. He would have tallied more goals had he played in more league matches.

QUICK FACT

Neymar scored two goals for Santos against Bolivar in a 2012 match. That made him the highest goal scorer for Santos since the legendary Pelé played for the team.

Opposing goalkeepers knew how they would spend some of their time when competing against Santos. They would be forced to dive in vain for soccer balls kicked by Neymar. His goals were not only frequent. They were amazing.

One of them was scored on September 26, 2012. About 33 scoreless minutes had been played in the Recopa Sudamericana final between Santos and the University of Chile. Neymar pulled up into an unguarded area in front of the left side of the net. A defender raced

Neymar battles for possession in the 2012 Recopa Sudamericana finals. He scored an incredible goal in that match against the University of Chile.

toward him from behind. Neymar passed the ball inside and cut over. He received the ball and booted it.

The Chile goalkeeper was guarding against a shot in that direction. It seemed he had cut off any shot to the left. But Neymar slammed the ball with such force and accuracy that it could not be stopped. The goalkeeper dove to his right and rolled over three times. The ball hit the net within inches of the left post.

Neymar raced to his right and hugged his teammates. He then broke into a dance. His celebration showed the joy he felt in scoring and a love for soccer.

That passion was one reason the best clubs in Europe were eager to sign him. The more important reason was his incredible talent. It motivated Barcelona to spend $76 million to lure him away from Santos when Neymar signed a five-year contract on May 27, 2013. He was introduced to Barcelona fans in June. The transfer was among the most expensive in soccer history.

Looking Toward the Future

The event was bittersweet for Neymar. He spoke about his love for the Santos fans. He thanked them for their loyalty. But he could not pass up the chance to compete with and against the top players in the world. One of them was Barcelona teammate and superstar Lionel Messi.

Neymar was jeered in his last match for Santos after announcing his departure. Fans booed when he got the ball and cheered when he lost it. He could take comfort that the match was not played in front of the Santos home fans. He tried to explain his motivation and praise what would soon be his former team.

"It was an honor to have played for this marvelous team, Santos," he said. "I am so happy I

Brazilian team star Neymar scores in a 2013 match against Spain. He would soon join the Spanish team FC Barcelona and become a star in Europe as well.

The incredible duo of Neymar and Lionel Messi celebrate after a victory. The FC Barcelona teammates joined forces to take the soccer world by storm.

did. Every child has a dream, either to be a player, a dentist, or a reporter. My dream was to become a professional athlete and I have achieved that. Today Barcelona is fulfilling my dream of going to a totally beautiful team."

QUICK FACT

No player benefitted more from the talent of Neymar than Barcelona teammate Lionel Messi. Neymar assisted on more Messi goals than any other Barcelona player.

Neymar vowed to return. He was moving to Spain, but he was still a Brazilian at heart. He proved it a month later when he played for its national team in the 2013 Confederations Cup final. Ironically, the opponent was Spain. Neymar performed brilliantly from beginning to end and scored a goal in a 3–0 victory. He was awarded the Golden Ball as the most valuable player in the tournament.

It took Neymar a little time to show his talent with Barcelona. He did not score in either of his first two matches with his new team. He finally booted one past the goalkeeper in his third match to help Barcelona clobber Thailand's national team 7–1 during Barcelona's 2013 tour of Asia. One of the assists belonged to Messi.

Future opponents cringed at the thought of trying to stop both Neymar and Messi. The pair soon began taking the soccer world by storm. But Neymar would never forget his roots. Brazil would continue to benefit from his greatness both on and off the soccer field.

CHAPTER THREE

From Star to Legend

No athletes can become superstars if they do not play on the big stage. FC Barcelona is among the greatest soccer clubs in the world. It competes in La Liga, the premier Spanish soccer league. Barcelona also plays against the top teams throughout Europe.

Superstars also become superstars in international events. The best players in Brazil are considered some of the best anywhere. They team up in the World Cup and Olympic Games. They compete against the greatest players assembled from every soccer-playing country.

By 2013, Neymar was playing for both Barcelona and the Brazilian national team. He was among the highest-paid athletes in the world. He had become a superstar. Now he set out to emerge as one of the greatest players in soccer history.

Neymar certainly had plenty of help with Barcelona. Playing on the same line as Messi and the brilliant Luis Suárez allowed him to maximize

QUICK FACT

Neymar played in at least 26 Spanish league matches for Barcelona in each of his first four seasons with the team. He scored an amazing 46 goals in 67 matches in the 2014–15 and 2015–16 seasons combined.

FC Barcelona fans root for Neymar and his teammates during a match against Spanish archrival Real Madrid.

his talent. However, his incredible quickness and ball-handling skills frequently required no assistance. He destroyed helpless defenders to score more than one goal every two games.

Neymar boots one past a sprawling goalkeeper in a 2015 La Liga match. His deadly shooting accuracy is one of his many attributes.

QUICK FACT

The most frequent victim of Neymar's goals was Villarreal and Atlético Madrid goalkeeper Sergio Asenjo. He was beaten six times by Neymar during Neymar's time with Barcelona.

Perhaps his best came in a La Liga match against Villarreal on November 8, 2015. Neymar faked out a defender by kicking the ball with his right foot to himself. He spun around the confused defender, then drilled the ball past a diving goalkeeper.

That was one of 105 goals Neymar scored for Barcelona in a four-year period. He became the second-highest scorer in FC Barcelona history among Brazilian players. In addition to the 105 goals he scored for the team, he added 59 assists. He tallied nearly one point per match.

But it was on the world stage for the Brazilian national team that Neymar made his biggest impact. His importance was most evident during the 2014 World Cup, which was hosted by Brazil. Neymar

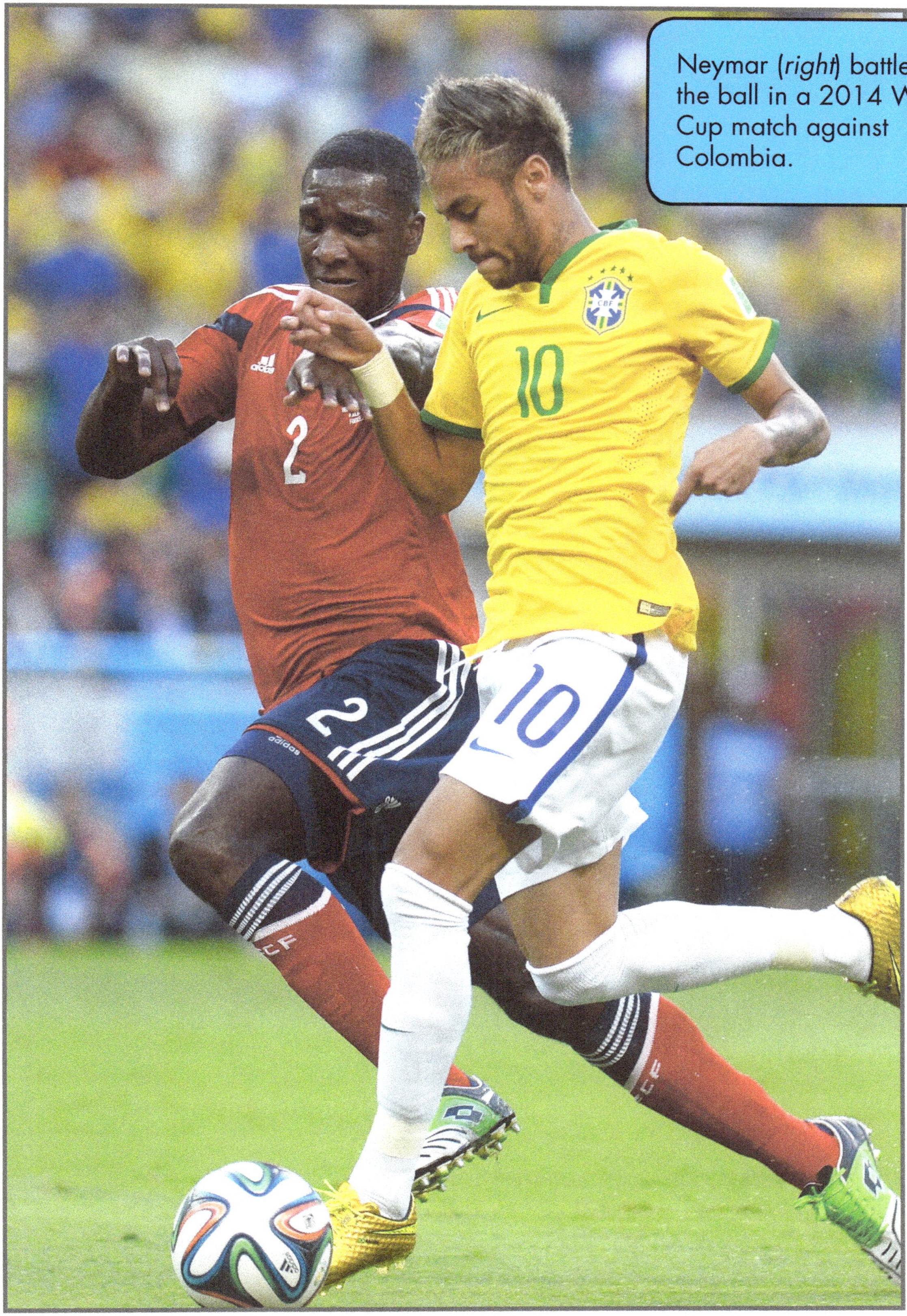

Neymar (*right*) battles for the ball in a 2014 World Cup match against Colombia.

QUICK FACT

Brazil had not hosted the World Cup in 64 years before the event came to that country in 2014. Its national team lost in the finals to fellow South American country Uruguay in 1950. But thereafter Brazil did win the World Cup five times. That number is the most of any country.

scored four goals in five matches to lead his team into the quarterfinals. But he broke a bone in his back during that match, a 2–1 victory for Brazil over Colombia on July 4.

Brazil was doomed without Neymar. It was clobbered by Germany, 7–1, in the semifinals. It also lost to the Netherlands, 3–0, in the third-place match.

Going for the Gold

The national team was luckier in the 2016 Summer Olympics. Neymar stayed healthy throughout. Brazil had never captured Olympic gold. It had placed second for the silver medal in 2012 and third for the bronze in 2008. Its fans were hoping Neymar could finally lead their team to a title, especially because the event was to be held in Brazil.

Neymar (*fourth from left*) joins his Brazilian teammates on the medal stand after winning Olympic gold in 2016. His game-winning goal proved the difference.

Neymar led the team with five of its eighteen goals. Brazil shut out all five opponents to reach the gold medal showdown against Germany on August 20, 2016. Brazil had a chance to avenge its 2014 World Cup defeat. The score was tied at 1–1 as the teams headed into a shoot-out to decide the winner. The shoot-out was knotted at 4–4 when Neymar lined up the ball in front of the net. He had already scored his team's only goal of the match.

A crowd of more than 63,000 at Maracana Stadium in Rio de Janeiro roared with excitement and anticipation. He took two steps forward, then stopped. He rushed toward the ball again. German goalkeeper Timo Horn guessed that Neymar would kick the ball to the Brazilian's left, so he dove in that direction. But Neymar had him fooled. He blasted the ball into the top-right corner of the goal.

Brazil had its first Olympic gold and Neymar had played the role of hero. He dropped to his knees and wept tears of joy as he was mobbed by his teammates. Never mind that he had joined Barcelona and left Santos. He was being cheered wildly by some of the same fans that had booed him only three years earlier.

A Brazilian flag was run from the stands into the group of rejoicing Brazilian players. When the celebration was over, Neymar spoke about his joy. He spoke about his love for Brazil. And he spoke about those that hated him for leaving.

"This is one of the best things that has happened in my life. That's it," he said. "Now my critics will have to shut up. I can't begin to describe my feelings. I have fulfilled my dream and to have fulfilled it in my home country makes me very proud."

Beating Paris, Joining Paris

A year later Neymar would be proud of another achievement. This time it was FC Barcelona that reaped the benefits of his greatness. It was March 8, 2017, when he exploded for three points in a matter of a few minutes in a Champions League match against Paris Saint-Germain. Each

Neymar (*right*) poses with his new jersey after signing a lucrative contract with Paris Saint-Germain. His arrival brought great joy and anticipation to his new team and its fans.

score was critical. Barcelona was down four goals after the first match of the knockout phase of the Champions League tournament. It needed to outscore its French foe by five to advance to the quarterfinals.

Time was running out. Only three minutes remained. Barcelona seemed lifeless. But Neymar remained full of life. He scored on an amazing free kick in which he curved the ball into the net from an incredible angle. He added another goal. Then he assisted on a Sergi Roberto goal to give Barcelona one of the greatest comeback victories in soccer history.

QUICK FACT

So excited was the Paris soccer club about the addition of Neymar that it released a video. It began with the words, "He's coming." It showed the famed Eiffel Tower in animated form with the colors of the Brazilian flag.

Little could Barcelona fans have imagined on that March day that Neymar would leave their team to join the one he had just beaten. He announced his decision to play for Paris Saint-Germain in July 2017. The deal would make him the highest paid soccer player ever.

The world soccer community was shocked. La Liga tried to block his transfer. FC Barcelona received $263 million from Paris Saint-Germain to complete it. But the Spanish soccer club sued him for breach of contract. FC Barcelona claimed that Neymar owed the team more money. The situation became a mess. As of December 2017 the lawsuit was still ongoing.

Neymar scored eight goals in eight games in 2017 for Paris Saint-Germain. He had started a new chapter in his life. He had gone from Brazil to Spain to France. Yet he never let go of his roots. He still loved Brazil. He cared about the nation in which he was born and raised. And he proved it with his heart and money.

CHAPTER FOUR

A Life Away from Soccer

It was June 2014. Soccer fans and teams were focused on the upcoming World Cup. Neymar yearned to turn that attention into help for his beloved Brazilian people. He was playing for FC Barcelona at the time. But he would never forget where he came from.

So Neymar came up with a plan. He would put his charitable side to work. He partnered with e-commerce

Neymar thrills a group of kids as he participates in a charity soccer match.

Singer Anitta performs with Neymar as the two launch a charity project in 2014. The Neymar Jr. Project Institute has provided kids with many opportunities to thrive.

QUICK FACT

Neymar is quite a religious Christian. He donates 10 percent of his income to his local church in Brazil.

company PayPal to launch an initiative, Competition for Good, to help bring badly needed clean water to his native country. All donations raised by the initiative would go to Waves for Water, a nonprofit organization that provides free water filters to communities in need.

Two days before Christmas of that year, the superstar launched the Neymar Jr. Project Institute. He had returned to the area near São Paulo in which he had spent much of his youth. His first task was to offer free classes to about 2,300 poor children in many sports and other activities. He yearned to provide opportunities for kids in need.

> **QUICK FACT**
>
> **More than 100,000 young players have taken part in an annual five-on-five soccer tournament run by Neymar's charity. The event helps raise money to help better the lives of Brazilian youth.**

His charity is based in the area in which he spent much of his childhood. But that area does not look the same as it did when he was young. The dump, where some of the locals were once forced to earn a living by helping recycling efforts, was closed. The district became cleaner and more modern.

A Changed Man

Starting such efforts helped Neymar grow as a person. So did becoming a father in August 2011. He had broken up with his former girlfriend, who was the mother of the child. But they both embraced their roles as parents. They named the boy David Lucca da Silva Santos. David split his time between his mother and father.

The responsibilities of fatherhood made a huge impact on Neymar. He had gained a reputation early in his career as lacking discipline off the field. His son changed all that.

"I have become much more mature," he said. "I did not know how to behave. But then I told myself that if I was man enough to make someone pregnant, I had to take my responsibility and act like a man. I have learned a lot from it and I am still learning things. My son David is the biggest joy in my life."

That says a lot given the joy he feels on the soccer field. Neymar turned that joy and talent into big money. That money has not come only

Neymar and his son, David Lucca, give a thumbs-up before a match. The responsibility of fatherhood and his love for his child helped change Neymar for the better.

from the teams for which he has played. He has become one of the most marketable athletes in the world.

Neymar earns millions in sponsorships every year. Among his corporate sponsors is the American sportswear giant Nike. He signed an 11-year contract with that company that pays him more than $100 million.

Neymar had become a very rich 25-year-old. He had gained sponsors from around the world. He helped sell shaving razors from Gillette. He hawked electronics from Panasonic and Beats by Dre. He pitched Red Bull energy drinks and Gaga Milano watches.

It was estimated in the summer of 2016 that Neymar earned $21 million annually from endorsements. These earnings made him the only active soccer player to make more money off the field than on it. It represented a bit more than three-fifths of his total income. But that was before he signed the lucrative deal with Paris Saint-Germain.

Neymar displays his gold Nike shoes during a match for FC Barcelona.

These defenders cannot stop Neymar from scoring for Paris Saint-Germain. Neymar made an immediate and positive impact on his new team.

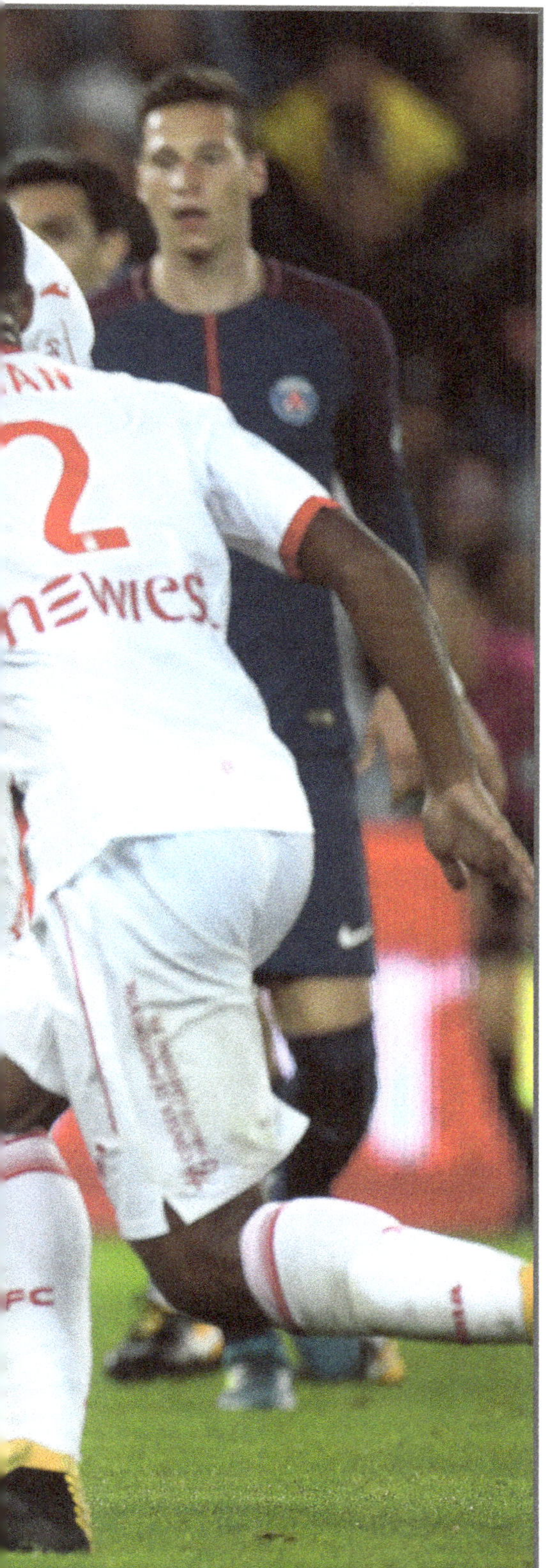

New Team, Same Greatness

That fortune would not have been possible without his incredible soccer talent. Neymar soon set out to help his new French team succeed. He got off on the right foot in his debut. He helped his team to a 3–0 win over host Guingamp. He earned Man of the Match honors with a goal and an assist.

Neymar appeared focused on his task from the start despite jeers from Guingamp fans before the match. He soon won over local fans. They gave him a standing ovation. And after the victory was achieved, he spoke about his career move.

"I knew it would be difficult to leave (Barcelona), but I'm very happy to be here," he said. "People believe that leaving Barca is like to die. But I'm more alive than ever. I'm very happy."

So was his team. Neymar shined again in his first home match for Paris Saint-Germain. He scored twice and aided in four other goals in a 6–2 win over Toulouse.

He saved his best for last. He brought the crowd to its feet with a goal that showed off his amazing ballhandling skills. He dribbled through a maze of defenders by changing directions. He rolled the ball off his foot left and right in an incredible display of balance. Then he booted the ball into the net. The feat was so amazing that even the Toulouse players lined up to shake his hand!

Many fans around the world, especially those that root for FC Barcelona, remained upset with Neymar for leaving that team. But nobody could question his talent and compassion.

Neymar had not only established himself as perhaps the greatest soccer player in the world. But he had proved his love and caring for the children of his home country. And his millions of fans could take heart in 2017 that he was only 25 years old. They could look forward to watching him play for many years to come.

TIMELINE

1992: Neymar da Silva Santos Jr. is born on February 5 near São Paulo, Brazil.

2003: Neymar joins FC Santos.

2009: Neymar makes his professional debut with Santos on March 7.

2010: Brazilian coach Dunga is criticized for leaving Neymar off the World Cup team. Neymar makes his debut with the Brazilian National Team on August 10.

2011: Neymar signs a lucrative sponsorship deal with Nike on March 24. He earns a spot on the Brazilian National Team on April 10. Neymar scores perhaps his greatest goal in July 27 against Flamengo. He becomes a father on August 24 as his son, David, is born. Neymar wins South American Footballer of the Year Award on September 20.

2012: Neymar is named to the Brazilian Olympic squad on May 11. He scores his 100th career goal for Santos on June 1. In December, Neymar wins the Golden Boot award for the second time, with 43 goals.

2013: FC Barcelona signs Neymar to a contract on May 27. In June, Neymar wins the Golden Ball for his performance in the Confederations Cup. Neymar scores his first goal for Barcelona on August 7 in defeat of Thailand.

2014: Back injury knocks Neymar out of 2014 World Cup. Neymar wins 2014 Bronze Boot Award in July. He scores four goals in one game on October 14 in defeat of Japan.

2016: Neymar scores winning shoot-out goal on August 20 to give Brazil the Olympic gold medal.

2017: Barcelona transfers Neymar to Paris Saint-Germain on August 2. Neymar scores his first goal for Paris Saint-Germain on August 13.

OTHER LIVING LEGENDS OF SOCCER

Pelé (1940–) is arguably the greatest soccer player ever. He is also among the top ambassadors of the game. He played a major role on the Brazilian national teams that won World Cup crowns in 1958, 1962, and 1970.

Diego Maradona (1960–) is considered by most experts the best soccer player of the 1980s. The Argentinian competed for FC Barcelona and the Argentine National Team. His "Hand of God" goal during the 1986 World Cup remains a legendary moment in soccer history; on that play, he illegally hit the ball with his hand, but the referee mistakenly thought he had used his head (which is allowed).

Mia Hamm (1972–) helped place soccer on the sports map in the United States. The American was the first female international star of the sport. She was a standout on the US national team that won World Cup championships in 1991 and 1999. The team also captured Olympic gold medals in 1996 and 2004. She twice won FIFA World Player of the Year honors.

David Beckham (1975–) is a former captain of the British national team. He became famous for his bending free kicks for Manchester United and Real Madrid before signing with the Major Soccer League LA Galaxy and helping popularize soccer in the United States.

Gianluigi Buffon (1978-) is ranked among the premier goalkeepers in the history of soccer. The Italian superstar, who first played for Parma and who joined Serie A club Juventus in 2001, holds the record for the longest scoreless stretch in Serie A history. He did not concede a goal over a period of 974 consecutive minutes during the 2015–16 season. Buffon retired in 2017.

Cristiano Ronaldo (1985–) is a highly talented forward from Portugal who has starred for Real Madrid. He is considered among the most gifted players of his generation.

Marta (1986–) is considered by many the finest women's soccer player of all time. The Brazilian scored a world record 15 goals in FIFA Women's World Cup tournament play. Marta won FIFA World Player of the Year every year between 2006 and 2010 and helped the Brazilian national team earn silver medals in the 2004 and 2008 Summer Olympics.

Lionel Messi (1987–) is an Argentine-born forward who went on to star for FC Barcelona, as well as the national team of his native country. He has won 29 trophies for Barcelona and eight La Liga titles.

GLOSSARY

acceleration The act or process of moving faster.

agility The ability to move quickly and easily.

bittersweet Combining sadness and happiness.

discipline The ability to keep working at something that is difficult.

charitable Freely giving money, food, or other kinds of help to needy or sick people.

dump A place where waste is taken and left.

endorsement The act of publicly saying that you like or use a product or service in exchange for money.

forward A player who plays near the opponent's goal.

free kick A kick that is awarded for fouls or violations of rules; when a free kick is taken, all players of the offending side must be 10 yards from the ball. Free kicks may be either direct (from which a goal may be scored), for more serious fouls, or indirect (from which a goal cannot be scored), for lesser violations.

goalkeeper The player whose job is to prevent balls from entering the goal.

hone To make more intense or effective.

inferior Something of poor quality.

instill To cause someone to have a certain feeling or attitude.

intervention The act of becoming involved in something to have an influence on what happens.

intriguing Extremely interesting or fascinating.

league A group of sports teams that play against each other.

lucrative Worth a lot of money, often referring to a contract.

marketable Able to be sold: wanted by buyers or employers.

nonprofit Not existing or done for the purpose of making a profit.

professional A person who gets paid to participate in a sport or activity.

scout A person whose job is to search for talented athletes, performers, and so forth.

shoot-out A competition used to decide the winner of a match by giving each team five chances to kick the ball into the goal.

sponsorship An arrangement in which a sponsor agrees to give money to someone or something.

swagger A way of walking or behaving that shows you have a lot of confidence.

tournament A sports competition consisting of a series of games and involving a number of teams.

transfer A transaction in professional soccer in which a player is purchased by one team from another.

World Cup An international soccer event that is held every four years and is considered the most significant in the sport.

FOR MORE INFORMATION

Books

Brandon, Roy. *Neymar: The Children's Book*. North Charleston, SC: CreateSpace Independent Publishing Platform, 2016.

Burshtein, Karen. *Lionel Messi: Soccer's Top Scorer*. New York, NY: Britannica Educational Publishing, 2016.

Callow, Nick. *Neymar: The Ultimate Fan Book*. London, UK: Carlton Books, Ltd., 2017.

Christopher, Matt. *Great Americans in Sports: Mia Hamm*. New York, NY: Little Brown and Company, 2015.

Crisfield, Deborah W. *The Everything Kids' Soccer Book: Rules, Techniques, and More About Your Favorite Sport!* 3rd ed. Avon, MA: Adams Media, 2015.

Gifford, Clive. *The Kingfisher Soccer Encyclopedia*. New York, NY: Kingfisher, 2016.

Hoena, Blake. *National Geographic Kids Everything Soccer: Score Tons of Photos, Facts, and Fun*. Washington, DC: National Geographic Society, 2014.

Jökulsson, Illugi. *Messi, Neymar, and Suarez: The Barcelona Trio*. New York, NY: Abbeville Press Publishers, 2016.

Jökulsson, Illugi. *Neymar: The New Pelé*. New York, NY: Abbeville Press Publishers, 2015.

Jökulsson, Illugi. *Stars of World Soccer*. New York, NY: Abbeville Press Publishers, 2015.

Latham, Andrew. *Soccer Smarts for Kids: 60 Skills, Strategies, and Secrets*. Berkeley, CA: Rockridge Press, 2016.

Lloyd, Carli, and Wayne Coffey. *All Heart: My Dedication and Determination to Become One of Soccer's Best*. Boston, MA: Houghton Mifflin Harcourt, 2018.

Logothetis, Paul. *Cristiano Ronaldo: International Soccer Star*. Minneapolis, MN: SportsZone, 2016.

Morgan, Alex. *Breakaway: Beyond the Goal.* New York, NY: Simon & Schuster Books for Young Readers, 2017.

The Official 2014 FIFA World Cup Brazil Kids' Handbook. London, UK: Carlton Books, Ltd., 2014.

Preminger, Tanya. *Sean Goes to Barcelona. A Children's Book About Soccer and Goals.* North Charleston, SC: CreateSpace Independent Publishing Platform, 2016.

Whiting, Jim. *FC Barcelona*. Mankato, MN: Creative Paperbacks, Inc., 2017.

Websites

FC Barcelona
https://www.fcbarcelona.com/neymar

Mirror
http://www.mirror.co.uk/all-about/neymar

Paris Saint-Germain
https://en.psg.fr/pro/stories/story/neymar-jr-a-paris

Who Scored?
https://www.whoscored.com/Players/50835/Show/Neymar

INDEX